BOOKS AND LIBRARIES

by Jack Knowlton   pictures by Harriett Barton

 HarperCollins*Publishers*

Library of Congress Cataloging-in-Publication Data

Knowlton, Jack.

    Books and libraries / by Jack Knowlton ; pictures
by Harriett Barton.

       p.   cm.

    Summary: A history of books and libraries from their beginnings in
Babylon, Egypt, and China, through the Greeks and the Middle Ages,
to the present day.

    ISBN 0-06-021609-3. — ISBN 0-06-021610-7 (lib. bdg.)

    1. Books—History—Juvenile literature   2. Libraries—History—
Juvenile literature. [1. Books—History. 2. Libraries—History.]
I. Barton, Harriett, ill. II. Title.

Z4.Z9K68   1991   89-70804

002—dc20   CIP

                                           AC

1 2 3 4 5 6 7 8 9 10

First Edition

Southern France
About 30,000 Years Ago

Long, long ago, people had tribal stories and legends they wanted to save and pass down to their children and grandchildren.

But 30,000 years ago no one could write down these stories, because writing, just like the wheel, had yet to be invented.

Some early ancestors of ours learned how to record their stories by painting pictures on the walls of their caves. They mixed charcoal, berry juices, and animal fats together to make paint. Then, by flickering lamplight, they painted beautiful pictures of wild animals and hunters throwing spears.

Writing would later be invented by different people, at different times, in different parts of the world.

River Valleys Around the World
About 8,000 Years Ago

About 8,000 years ago most people lived in small wandering tribes. They survived by hunting, fishing, and gathering wild plants.

But some tribes were slowly changing the way they lived. They moved into river valleys around the world and became farmers and shepherds. They grew wheat, corn, and rice. They raised sheep, goats, and chickens.

Over time the tribes built villages and towns. For the first time ever, large groups of people were living and working together. Civilization had begun.

With the coming of civilization people soon had a practical, everyday need to write. As a result, the earliest forms of writing were probably *symbols* for counting, measuring, and keeping track of things.

People counted and recorded the passing days and made calendars. Farmers counted the bushels of grain they grew and sold. Bakers counted the loaves of bread they baked.

Mesopotamia   About 5,000 Years Ago

morning

five oxen

A people named the Sumerians moved into Mesopotamia, the land between the Tigris and Euphrates rivers, about 3,000 B.C. Today this area is a hot, dry desert in southern Iraq, but five thousand years ago it was full of cool running waters.

The Sumerians farmed the rich land, built the world's first cities, and invented a simple *picture writing*. A picture of the rising sun meant morning. A picture of an ox with five dots beneath it meant five oxen.

The Sumerians made the world's first books. They etched pictures on flat slabs or *tablets* of soft, damp clay. Then the tablets were baked in ovens until they were as hard as rocks. Each tablet was a page in a book.

Later the pictures were replaced with little triangular marks made by pressing sharpened pieces of river reed into the clay. This new way of writing was easier and faster.

ox   *sun*   *grain*

The Sumerians built libraries to store their books. The hard, but easily broken, tablets were carefully tied together with twine or neatly stacked in baskets by librarians called the Keepers of the Tablets.

In modern times, thousands of perfectly preserved Sumerian tablets have been found beneath the dry desert sands.

Egypt   About 5,000 Years Ago

The ancient Egyptians created a great civilization on the banks of the Nile River. They invented a beautiful, but difficult, picture language called *hieroglyphics.*

Specially trained writers or *scribes* painted hieroglyphics on a kind of paper called *papyrus.* The stalk of the papyrus plant, a reed that grows in swamps near the Nile, was carefully split open and flattened down to make this "paper."

Almost all the scribes worked for the rulers of ancient Egypt, who were called the Pharaohs. So almost all the early rolls of papyrus were kept in libraries in the Pharaohs' palaces, temples, and tombs.

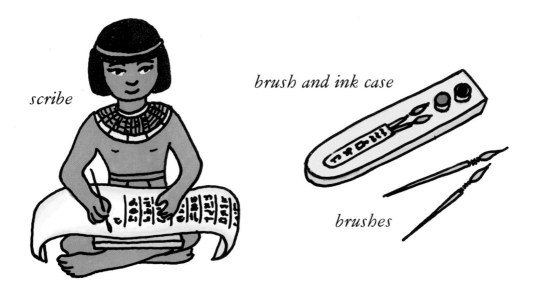

scribe

brush and ink case

brushes

Much later the Egyptians developed a simpler form of writing. It was called *popular writing*, and was much easier for people to read and write. Soon there were many more papyrus books and many private libraries.

But papyrus becomes as dry and delicate as a dead leaf over time, so nearly all the early Egyptian books have long since turned to dust and joined the shifting sands of the desert.

The world's first sheets of real paper were made from a smelly
pulp of wood chips, cotton rags, and even old fishing nets.

China   About 5,000 Years Ago

China's civilization, like many others, grew alongside its many rivers, especially the mighty Yangtze and the Huang Ho, or Yellow River.

The ancient Chinese also wrote with a simple picture language. Over the centuries they improved and added to this language, which they still use today.

earth

The Chinese used mink- or camel-hair brushes and a shiny black ink to paint *pictograms*, or word pictures, on flat pieces of wood or bamboo. They often painted their poetry on panels of pure silk cloth.

water

But silk was too rare and expensive to be widely used, so the Chinese looked for a less expensive writing material. They finally found it in the year A.D. 105, when a government official named Ts'ai Lun invented paper. The Chinese managed to keep the art of papermaking a secret for over 700 years.

fire

The Imperial Library, the largest and finest in China, belonged to the Emperor of China. It lay behind the high walls that surrounded the Emperor's palace and its grounds—a place called, with awe, the Forbidden City.

Young Greeks went to excellent schools called *academies*.

Greece   1600 B.C. to 146 B.C.

Α
Β
Γ
Δ
Ε
Ζ
Η
Θ
Ι
Κ
Λ
Μ
Ν
Ξ
Ο
Π
Ρ
Σ
Τ
Υ
Φ
Χ
Ψ
Ω

Although ancient Greece was a very small country, it was one of the greatest empires in the ancient world. It was the birthplace of Western civilization.

The Greeks had a written language that used an *alphabet* of 24 letters instead of pictures. The Greeks wrote on papyrus imported from Egypt. They wrote with quill pens made from the feathers of eagles, ravens, and geese.

The Greeks wanted their citizens to read and write and think clearly. For the first time in history, reading and writing became popular.

The Greeks filled their many libraries with rolls and scrolls about science, geography, arithmetic, and the dramatic myths of their gods and goddesses.

The Greeks spread their culture and learning far beyond the borders of their own country. They started more schools and built more libraries than anyone else in the ancient world.

They built the most famous of all ancient libraries in a city on the northern coast of Egypt. The city was named Alexandria to honor the legendary Greek military leader Alexander the Great.

Alexandria, Egypt   300 B.C. to A.D. 642

The great library at Alexandria existed for over 900 years. Stacked on its shelves were about 700,000 scrolls—equal to 100,000 modern books. It was the largest, finest, and most valuable collection of books in the world.

The librarians at Alexandria wanted their collection to include a copy of *every* important book ever written. So soldiers searched for books on every ship that anchored in the busy harbor at Alexandria. They seized any rare books they found and took them to the great library to be copied.

Around 200 B.C. the king of Egypt stopped the export of papyrus from his country. Without papyrus, people in other lands couldn't make books. Some say the Egyptian king was jealous of a new library in the city of Pergamum in Turkey. He feared this new library might rival, or even outshine, his library at Alexandria.

The librarians at Pergamum reacted by finding a substitute for papyrus. They perfected the use of animal skins as writing surfaces when they invented *parchment*. Now they could make new books even without papyrus from Egypt.

Parchment was made by splitting the skin of a goat or sheep, bleaching it white, pounding it flat, and rubbing it smooth.

Rome and its Empire
200 B.C. to A.D. 476

By 150 B.C., the armies of Rome had conquered Greece. The victorious Romans adopted many Greek ideas, including the idea of public libraries.

The Romans built handsome libraries throughout their vast empire. Most Roman libraries had two reading rooms. In one room all the books were written in Greek. In the other room the books were written in Latin, the language of Rome.

Roman librarians stored their papyrus and parchment scrolls in pigeonhole cupboards that were nailed to the walls. Especially rare and valuable scrolls were locked away in heavy oak chests that were lined with fragrant cedarwood to ward off insects and mold.

The Romans replaced the scroll with the *codex*. Its pages were sewn together and bound between covers just like this book.

The citizens of Rome were proud of their libraries. But their books and libraries were only as safe as the Roman Empire itself, and the Empire had many enemies. Eventually waves of barbarian armies swept down from the dark forests of the north. And when the once-mighty Roman Empire weakened and finally fell, a Dark Age slowly covered Europe.

The work of copying old books and slowly filling empty library shelves was a never-ending task.

Europe   A.D. 500 to 1000

Europe's Dark Age lasted about five hundred years. It was a dangerous time. Law and order disappeared. War and crime were common. Schools were neglected and closed. Books and libraries were destroyed.

But here and there, in small religious communities called *monasteries*, monks began to save the almost-forgotten wisdom of ancient Greece and Rome. They searched for copies of the old, important books, and from them made new hand-written copies, or *manuscripts*.

The monks copied the old books, letter by letter, onto fine parchment. The work was difficult, but they were dedicated.

The monks copied from dawn to dusk, six days a week, in rooms neither heated nor lit by candles, for fear of fire. A large volume could take a year or more to complete and could require the skins of 200 sheep.

 After the Dark Ages came a period of history we call the Middle Ages. By then the monks were adding beautiful art to their manuscripts. Their pages were *illuminated*—made bright and radiant—with color and gold decoration.

Europe   A.D. 1000 to 1500

Toward the end of the Middle Ages there was an exciting, creative period called the *Renaissance*, or rebirth. People were enthusiastic about learning again. Schools and colleges opened. People wanted to read. People wanted books.

But there were very few books to go around. There were no public libraries left, and most private libraries filled only a single shelf.

There were now professional scribes copying books. They worked in teams and copied faster, but not as neatly, as the monks. Hand copying books was always slow, hard work.

During the Middle Ages some books were also made with *woodcut printing*, a method invented by the Chinese. With

woodcuts many copies of a page could be printed on paper.

But woodcuts allowed for only a few hand-carved words and a picture on each page, so they were mostly used for short prayer books and children's schoolbooks. And since each page had to be carefully, and patiently carved, it too was an awfully slow way to make books.

Books were so few and so valuable that some were bound between heavy metal covers and chained to the walls of churches and college libraries.

Mainz, Germany   A.D. 1400 to 1500

Around the year 1400, a boy was born in Germany and named Johannes Gensfleisch, which means John Gooseflesh. He later changed his last name to Gutenberg, which means Good Mountain.

We know very little about the life of Johannes Gutenberg—we don't even know what he looked like. But we do know the world was changed forever because of his life and the genius of his work.

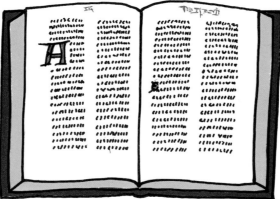

By 1450, after years of trial and error, Gutenberg invented a method of printing books using a printing press and small movable pieces of metal type.

Once a page of type was set, letter by letter and word by word, it was locked into place, and ink was rolled onto the type. Then a printer and his press could quickly and easily print thousands of exact copies of that page.

With Gutenberg's invention a printer and his press could produce thousands of copies of a book in the time it took a monk to copy just one!

In Europe, printed books were soon plentiful, widely available, and much less expensive than manuscripts. People and libraries could easily buy books for the first time in history.

Colonial New England   Early 17th Century

In 1620 the first Pilgrims left England for America. They boarded a little ship named the *Mayflower* and sailed west across the Atlantic. After a stormy trip they landed on the rocky coastline of New England and named their settlement the Massachusetts Bay Colony.

Other Pilgrims soon followed. Like all pioneers, they could bring only those things most needed to settle a new land—pigs, goats, pots, pans, rifles, tools, and farm equipment. Books would be a luxury until they had cleared the forests, built houses and barns, and planted and harvested crops.

In those early days there were no real libraries in New England, only small family book collections that were shared with friends and neighbors.

In 1638 the first printing press in America was shipped from England. It was soon at work in the new town of Cambridge, Massachusetts. In the same year, in the same town, the first American college, Harvard College, was given 380 books to start a library. The Harvard Library was the first true library in the United States.

Family book collections included Bibles, Greek and Roman literature, and practical handbooks about law, medicine, seamanship, and farming.

Colonial Philadelphia
Early 18th Century

In 1718, a twelve-year-old boy began work as a printer's "devil" or apprentice. The boy's name was Benjamin Franklin.

Though Franklin is best remembered for his many other occupations—inventor, statesman, philosopher, scientist—his first loves would always be books and printing.

Franklin opened his own printing shop in Philadelphia at the age of twenty-two. Over the next forty years he printed newspapers, paper money, and hundreds of books, including his own famous book, *Poor Richard's Almanac.*

In 1731 Franklin had one of his many good ideas. He began the world's first "subscription library." The idea was simple. Franklin and about fifty of his friends each paid in a small sum of money that was pooled together to buy books. Then any "subscriber" could borrow a book or two at a time.

Franklin's library, the Library Company of Philadelphia, was very popular. It quickly added new members and was copied in other cities in both America and Europe. The "Library Company" is still open and lending books in Philadelphia today.

Franklin wrote and published books, and he and his wife, Deborah, sold books in their bookstore.

The United States　Early 19th Century

The United States became a free and independent nation on July 4, 1776. On that warm and sunny summer day the Declaration of Independence was signed in Philadelphia.

Over the next hundred years some Americans had a good library nearby, but most lived far from any library at all.

In the towns of New England small "social libraries" opened in the early 1800s. Many got started with donations of used books. Most soon closed their doors for lack of money.

Other libraries survived by copying Franklin's idea of charging a small membership fee. One of these—the Bingham Library for Youth—was the world's first library built especially for children. It opened its doors in Salisbury, Connecticut, in 1803. It's still open and still full of children and books.

America's oldest free public library is in the small town of Peterborough, New Hampshire. It began in 1833 with just a few bookshelves in the town's combination general store, library, and post office. The Peterborough Public Library is still open today.

The American Frontier   19th Century

The United States grew as people headed west to the frontier. First came the explorers and mapmakers. Then came pioneer families who traveled west on foot, on horseback, and in covered wagons.

For the first few years on the frontier, books were a great luxury. But once life became safe and secure, people wanted the things they'd done without for so long, including books.

But since the libraries and bookstores were "way back East," people had to find ways to get books to the pioneer men, women, and children who now lived "out West."

Some early pioneers in Ohio wanted books to read, but they didn't have much money. So they founded "Coonskin Libraries"—subscription libraries that accepted raccoon pelts as membership fees.

Later, one New York publisher sold a series of schoolbooks called the "Library in a Box." About fifty books were shipped out west in a sturdy pinewood box that became a four-shelf bookcase when nailed to the wall of a frontier schoolhouse.

And until bookstores and libraries were common in the West, general stores often had a few books for sale. They sat on shelves between sacks of sugar and bolts of calico.

The Dewey Decimal number for this book is 002.

The United States   Turn of the Century

America's Centennial was in 1876. On July Fourth of that year, the United States was 100 years old. Eighteen seventy-six was also the year when a young man named Melvil Dewey began a long career that would soon make him America's most famous librarian.

Melvil Dewey was full of good ideas about how to improve America's libraries. He founded the first college of library science, the first state library, and some of the first horse-drawn traveling libraries.

When Dewey began his work, most American libraries were badly organized. Every library had its own system of shelving books. Sometimes books were shelved by size, sometimes by the author's last name, and sometimes by the color of the cover! It was all very confusing.

Dewey ended the confusion with his most famous idea: the Dewey Decimal System, or Dewey Code. This system gives every nonfiction book a code number according to its subject, so it can be shelved in order. For example, books about earthquakes have Dewey Decimal number 551.21, and rodeos have 791.8.

Dewey's shelving system was very popular and successful, and is used in over 100 countries today.

Scotland and America
19th and 20th Centuries

As a young boy, Andrew Carnegie emigrated from Scotland to America with his parents in 1848. He was soon working, at the age of thirteen, as a "bobbin boy" in a cotton mill in Allegheny, Pennsylvania. His salary was $1.20 per week.

Carnegie always loved to read, but Allegheny, like most small towns, didn't have a public library then. But Carnegie was lucky. A leading citizen of the town, Colonel Anderson, had an excellent private library, which he let the neighborhood children use on Saturday afternoons. Andrew was there every Saturday.

In the years that followed, Carnegie became one of the richest men in America. From 1880 to the end of his life in 1919, he spent much of his time giving his money away.

He gave millions of dollars to build museums, colleges, and concert halls. He loved the sound of organ music, so he donated over 7,000 pipe organs to churches and synagogues.

Andrew Carnegie never forgot the example set by Colonel Anderson. He spent many millions of dollars to build over 2,500 free public libraries in the United States, Canada, England, and his birthplace, Scotland.

Washington, D.C.   1800 to the Present

The Library of Congress in Washington, D.C., is America's national library. It began, in 1800, as a small government library in the U.S. Capitol building.

The original Library of Congress and all its books were destroyed when the Capitol building was burned to the ground by the British army in the War of 1812. A new and better library was soon begun when Congress purchased about 7,000 books from the collection owned by President Thomas Jefferson.

The Library grew slowly but steadily for the next sixty years. Then, in 1870, Congress passed a law that two copies of

every book printed and copyrighted in the United States must be donated to the Library of Congress. After this, the Library grew rapidly.

The Library moved into its own beautiful building in 1897. A million books—weighing 800 tons—were moved by wheelbarrows and horse-drawn wagons from the Capitol to the new building. The Library now fills three huge buildings.

Today, the Library of Congress is the largest library in the world. It contains millions of maps, movies, and manuscripts and over 20 million books in 470 languages on 535 miles of bookshelves.

Today   Your Neighborhood Library

From the clay tablets of ancient Sumeria to the computers in modern libraries, the purpose of books and libraries hasn't changed at all.

Books and libraries are the memory of mankind. They are the storehouses of human thought and imagination.

Nothing is hidden from you in the library. Books contain wisdom and wit, facts and fantasy, for young and old alike.

With a book in your hand you can look into the past and even catch glimpses of the future.

MELVIL DEWEY'S

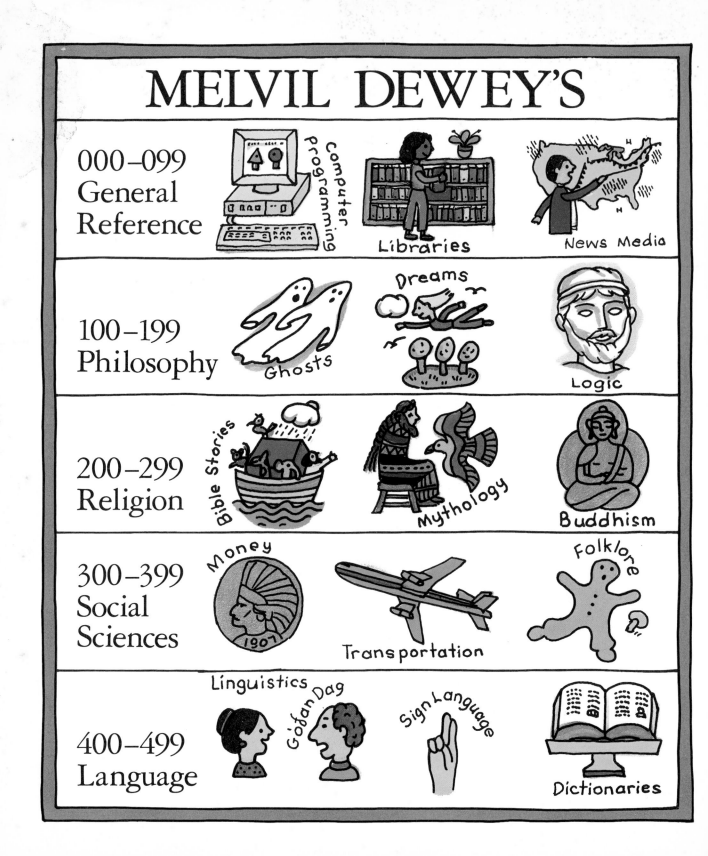

000–099 General Reference	Computer programming · Libraries · News Media
100–199 Philosophy	Ghosts · Dreams · Logic
200–299 Religion	Bible Stories · Mythology · Buddhism
300–399 Social Sciences	Money · Transportation · Folklore
400–499 Language	Linguistics · Góðan Dag · Sign Language · Dictionaries